LIVING THE LIFE OF A WORSHIPPER

Sabrina A. Shaw

Sabrina A. Shaw
Farmingville, New York

Copyright © 2019 Sabrina A. Shaw. All rights reserved. No part of this publication may be reproduced, stored in or introduced into a retrieval system, or transmitted, in any form or by any means (electronic, mechanical, photocopying, recording or otherwise), without the prior written permission of the copyright owner. The scanning, uploading, and distribution of this book via the Internet or any other means without the permission of the publisher are illegal and punishable by law. Please purchase only authorized electronic editions and do not participate in or encourage electronic piracy of copyrighted materials. Your support of the author's rights is appreciated.

Limits of Liability ~ Disclaimer

The author and publisher shall not be liable for your misuse of this material. This book is strictly for informational purposes. The author and publisher do not guarantee that anyone following the techniques, suggestions, tips, ideas, or strategies will become successful. The author and publisher shall have neither liability nor responsibility to anyone concerning any loss or damage caused, or alleged to be caused, directly or indirectly by the information contained in this book.

Scripture References: www.biblegateway.com unless otherwise stated, all scriptures are quoted from New King James Bible.

Cover Design – Vision Works
Editing-Interior Layout – The Self-Publishing Maven
Formatting – Istvan Szabo, Ifj., Sapphire Guardian International
Photography – Eli
ISBN 13: 978-0-578-46852-5
Printed in the United States of America

ACKNOWLEDGMENTS

I must begin by giving God thanks. My relationship with Him is how my worship was birthed. God, I praise you for the freedom to worship and for blessing me with the ability to use my gift, talent, and ability to sing songs of worship. When I think about Your goodness, I shake my head when I look back from where You brought me.

My parents Ellis and Tommie Billings, I thank you for giving me life. Mommy thank you for being a stern parent and making me go to church when I didn't want to. Even when I would move slow and think it was too late for church, you drove fast to get us there on time. Daddy, I miss you terribly, but I'm grateful that we were able to worship together before the Lord called you home. You sir became a fan of the word of God, and for that I'm grateful.

My sisters, Phyllis, Jeannette and Dorothy, who exemplifies "a family that prays together, stays together. Not only are we together, we all are serving in our churches. I love you ladies to life. Don't Stop.

The best In-Loves anyone could ask for, Rudolph and Gwenda Shaw. Mom and Dad, I love you. Because of you I have two mothers, and gained another father. Your love for God and each other encourages me every day.

My children, Alonzo (Lonnie), Shauntae (Tae Tae Mama), and Jonathan, Jr (JJ). My heart, my loves, and my everything, I love you so much. Alonzo, you were there in the beginning stages of my worship with God. Tae you were there during my growing stages of my worship with God. JJ, you are there in my matured stages of my worship with God. Thank you for being a part of one the most important parts of my life. Let's continue to worship together.

Jonathan Shaw, Sr. what can I say? Actually, there is much to say and there are not enough words or pages to express my love. You have been my greatest encourager from day one. I've never met anyone like you, and I'm so happy to say I'm married to you. When I began to understand what worship really was and I had questions about all the emotions I was going through, you were patient with me to explain it all. Not only that, you would worship with me. Real men worship! Your love for God, has honestly kept me. Walking with you on this journey of life is more than I could have ever asked for. Thank you for being my champion and example of worship in human form. I love you my dear.

Thank you Robin Devonish. Not only are you my publisher, adjutant and friend, but the one who encouraged me to write this book. You shared how you have gleaned from my worship and thought that others should know more about me and my worship. Robin, thank you so much for encouraging me to write this book, and for helping me bring this to fruition. Blessings to you always.

All my nieces, nephews, and family; let's live a life of worship, and please God together.

God Bless You All!

FOREWORD

Bible scholars and theologians use a term called the law of the first mentioned. It is a method by which researchers determine the origin of a thing based upon when it was first mentioned in the Bible. This will then give us a clear direction of what God originally intended when something is mentioned for the first time in scripture.

Let's look at when worship was first mentioned in the Bible. Worship occurred in Genesis 22:3-10. Now certainly the worship of gods and even unto God was going on before this time, but again it is when it was first mentioned not when it first occurred. Factually, worship first occurred in the garden with Adam and Eve. Their mere existence was within itself worship. But after the fall of man the first time worship is mentioned is in Genesis 22 in the story of Abraham and Isaac.

Then on the third day, Abraham lifted up his eyes, and saw the place afar off. And Abraham said unto his young men, Abide ye here with the ass; and I and the lad will go yonder and worship, and come again to you. Genesis 22:4-5

In this story, there was no mention of keyboards, drums, guitars, no choirs, nor any singers or dancers. It is just Abraham and his son, going to the place where the Lord showed him, to worship. Instead, in this story, there is an altar, and a sacrifice and someone's heart turned towards the obedience of God.

What can we learn from this? We learn that worship is not so much what we do with our lips but rather what we do with our lives based upon the positioning of our heart! In Romans 12 Apostle Paul encourages us to offer our lives as a living sacrifice. To limit worship to a moment in a church service, which mostly occurs once a week, is an incredible insult to the object of your worship.

So we must breakdown several interesting points to ensure our worship is proper. Jesus tells the Samaritan woman in John 4 that true worship is to the Father in spirit and in truth. Jesus not only tells this woman what worship is, but He makes a differentiation between true and false worship. Let's examine this in three parts:

1. The object of worship
2. The motivation to worship
3. The method of worship

The first is the object of your worship. We must make this very clear today because people worship many things and many people. The dictionary definition of the word worship means to reverence and pay homage to God or a sacred person or to any object that is regarded sacred. The dictionary admits that God is not the only one worshipped. Today, people worship money, possessions, relationships, animals, astrology and even the devil. Whatever you esteem above yourself and you give extreme reverential attention to… you worship! Now, this is not to be confused with honor. Honor isn't worship. However, honor is an ingredient in worship. We will get more to that later. To be effective in your worship, you must know the object of your worship. Who is your worship directed toward? In a world where we can be unfocused and scattered in our thinking, focus is essential in worship.

Focus allows us to stay on target as to whom this reverence, honor, and esteem is going toward. When we dissect the word HALLELUJAH, it is a perfect expression of worship. I know many categorize this word with praise only, but it is certainly a word that expresses worship. The prefix HALLE is a word meaning worship. It means to be hilarious or lose ones-self. The next syllable LU means towards or directed. The suffix JAH is an abbreviation or a term for Jehovah God. So the full word HALLELUJAH means to be hilarious towards God! This word states that God is the object and the focus of our worship. Which means this word should only be used for God.

The next part is the motivation to worship. In Genesis, Abraham was willing to sacrifice his only son Isaac. This speaks to the position and the condition of his heart. One of the reasons why some people aren't effective in worship is because their heart is not properly motivated. Believe it or not, people worship so that they can say they did. Some people even worship because they like to be associated with God. But God isn't really worshipped in these encounters because He isn't the focus or the motivation as to why they are doing it. Some people even worship out of religious practice. That means that if it is a habit for you to go to church on Sunday, you do it because of tradition. You may be in the church, but you have yet to worship. Your heart isn't in it! It is imperative to examine your motivation or your heart in worship. The scripture in John 4 again states in spirit and in truth. The truth part speaks to the positioning of your heart. There's a pure element of honesty necessary to truly worship. Matthew 15:8 states "This people draw near to me with their mouth, and honor me with their lips; but their heart is far from me." You can't worship God without a heart towards God.

Lastly, I want to highlight the method of worship. Now I don't want you to confuse method with style. There are many different styles of worship due to culture differences and societal changes. A style can be a cultural expression. And because we are very different people there will be different styles of worship. But the method speaks to something a bit deeper and more general for everyone to apply. The method speaks to the manner you employ to carry out your worship. Let's take another look again at Abraham in Genesis 22. He told his servants that he and his son were going to worship. The word worship there is Shachah. Shachah means to bow down and reverence. He stated that he and his son were going to bow down and reverence God.

Throughout all of scripture when anyone went to worship God, it was either audible or visible. There is no such thing as to worship in your heart, but your mouth and body don't get the message. Worship is heard or seen... or both! Because God is the object of our worship and our worship comes from the position of our heart, the immediate response is a verbal expression of worship or an act of worship. Let's explore a few of these to get a sense of different methods of worship. Here are a few Hebraic words and what they mean for worship:

- HALLAH – To boast or brag about God until it becomes foolish. Psalm 63:3-4 (This is the word mentioned before in HALLELUJAH)
- YADAH – Means to extend your hands. Psalm 134:2
- BARAK – Used to denote blessings. Psalm 34:1
- TEHILLAH – To sing or to laud. Psalm 22:3
- ZAMAR – To pluck the strings of an instrument. Psalm 18:1-3
- TODAH – To shout with a grateful attitude even in need. Psalm 56
- SHABACH – To shout with a loud voice. Daniel 4:37

Worship is essential to the life of the believer. Don't get caught up in the music, but music is good. Don't become dependent upon the atmosphere of the church, but the church atmosphere is good. But worship is your life! When worship becomes how you live, and you choose to live a life of worship, you will begin to develop a relationship with God that is out of this world. Worship isn't what you do; it's how you live. And your life will become so much better when God is the focus of your worship. Worship is how you wake up in the morning. Worship is how you take care of your body. Worship is you properly relating to your family. Worship is how you conduct yourself on your job. Worship is how you relate to the rest of the world and how you treat those you don't think you need. Jesus told the disciples in Matthew 25 "when you have done it unto the least of them, you have done it unto me." This is worship! Today choose to make worship your lifestyle instead of a religious act once a week.

Dr. Jonathan Shaw

Contents

A Little Bit About Me 13

Inner 25
    Self-Examination 27
    Prayer 31
    Repentance 35
    Humility 39
    Forgiveness 43
    Intimacy 47
    Healing 51
    Fearlessness 55
    Focused 59
    Truth 63
    Belief 67
    Unconditional Love 71

Outer 75
    Being an example 77
    Song of the Lord 81
    Reading the Word 85
    Patience 89

Time	93
Consistency	97
Balance	99
Family	103
Marriage	107
Fun	111
Encouragement	115

Community 119
Community	121
Connection	129
Giving	133
Support/Listening	137
Resources	139

Conclusion 143

A Little Bit About Me

What is worship? The feeling or expression of reverence and adoration for a deity.

I remember at the age of five going to church with my Aunt Sally. We went to Universal Temple on Eastern Parkway in Brooklyn, which was big and crowded. If I didn't hold my aunt's hand tight, I thought I'd get lost. One Sunday, I went with her and folks were clapping and shouting (I mean jumping up and down), and I asked her what were they doing. My aunt told me to sit there and be quiet, their worshipping God. That thing scared me to no end.

Listen, I was five years old, and no one told me what that was. Back then you did as you were told or a slap across came across the face. You didn't ask questions and my Aunt Sally was no one to play with.

Parts of my family were all about attending church. However, I felt something was missing. Although a close family, we didn't do church together. I didn't think about it much as to why I went and no one else in the house attended. Looking back on it now, it was an interesting situation. Sometimes my mother would go to church and leave me home. My father and my siblings didn't go at all. I would though hear stories that my older brother and sister played in a drum and buggle corp. on Sunday's sometimes. But church, nope!

Sometimes, I'd go with friends on the block where I lived in Brooklyn, and we visited different churches as well. I went to Baptist, Catholic and Methodist churches and those with no affiliation. They all had their set of rules and standards of worship.

One day I attended Trinity Baptist Church with my friend Shannon. I was singing along with them, and the choir director heard me singing. I guess I was loud. LOL. She asked me if I wanted to sing with the choir. I said, "Sure I'd love to, but do I have to join your church?" She said, "No." I agreed to join the choir.

When they had rehearsals, I would go and only attend church when I had to sing. I wasn't interested in God, just the opportunity to sing. The truth is, while in service, there were no praise breaks, no power (as I understand what it is today), just clapping. In my mind, there was nothing to draw me. No one tried to introduce me to God, they just liked my voice. As I think back, having influence over a 13 year old attending church could've been a good thing. Why didn't they try and get me to a place with God when it was clear I didn't have Him? Or were they convinced they saw was a young girl who already had a relationship with God? Was this all church was about? It felt empty, as if something was missing.

After visiting many churches, I thought I was getting closer to what I believed worship was, in the form of singing. When I began attending Norman Thomas High School, I joined the gospel choir. Mr. Ramon Reeberg, who I'm still in communication with today, was my choir director. He was tough on us, pushing us to sing with technique and from our gut. That was his job, but he also cared about us. Then there was Ms. Rose Canty who was my sister's music teacher when she went to the same school; Ms. Canty was instrumental in helping me to further develop my voice.

At first I didn't lead a song, I wasn't in the front, nor did I want to be. I sang in the back and liked it. One of my choir mates Kim Neal went to church and would talk to me about God and how wonderful He was. There was something different about Kim; she wasn't like all the others who sang. She didn't curse, smoke, or drink. You could tell she loved the God she spoke about.

I would listen to her because she made God sound interesting. I wondered how she knew so much and who told her about God. Maybe if I joined her church someone would be there to tell me, teach me. Then one day at a performance, she started crying during a song, and then I started crying because I saw her crying. Suddenly, I felt different. I didn't equate it with worship at the time so it had to be my emotions. I couldn't control my tears. This experience didn't happen often, but I did wonder every time we went out to sing, whether or not those emotions would come back.

Since my visits to church were few and far between, the experiences were as well. Worship was still a mystery to me. I did experience the tears again, but only when the choir sang and I saw others get emotional. Those were the people who went to church regularly.

As time went on, I figured out what praise was because it was all around me and expressed openly. Praise was also done with the feet and hand clapping. I even learned a pretty good dance. I praised God without being in a church service. It didn't matter what day of the week or where I was, I could praise God. I'd praise Him because of His goodness.

Side bar: Can you imagine driving your car and just thanking God? Wow, the many times I had to pull my car over. As I write this, the flashback I'm having of the time I heard "I Won't Complain" for the first time. The tears that flowed from my eyes were uncontrollable. It was wonderful to feel God's love through song. Even though I was told singing wasn't going to save me, I believe it did. Singing saved my life. Then I finally asked myself, is this worship?

Back to the story...
Then suddenly, the day came where I was introduced to worship.

I finally joined a church. My mother took me to St. Paul Church of Christ Disciples of Christ when I was 14 years old. At first I didn't like it because I never saw any young people; just a bunch of people my mother's age. There were three choirs, and every time I'd go to church my thoughts were, 'where are the young people?' Until one Sunday I saw different. There were more people in the choir stand and they were in my age group. I was excited! Yes, this was right up my alley. After service my mother introduced me to family members I'd never met. My cousin Yvette was the organist for the three choirs in that church. When I met her, I thought 'she reminds me of Kim from my school choir.' She seems to love God too.

In addition to meeting family, I met the organist of the young people's choir. His name was Eddie Moses and the choir was The Youth for Christ. Eddie asked me if I could sing, and encouraged me to join. I thought, 'Not again, another choir.' I hesitated at first but agreed to join not knowing my yes would put me in the front.

The next Sunday he asked me to sing a solo, I did and many said they were blessed. I met some wonderful people who loved God. Eddie must have known what I needed because he introduced me to Lynda Harper. Lynda to me was the perfect example of someone who loved God. Between Kim and Lynda, I wanted to do right around them. At church, I had Lynda, Frank Webster, Anthony Slayter and Chuck staying on me to make sure I got saved. They didn't want me lost. On a consistent basis they spoke to me about giving my life to the Lord. When I tell you, they spoke to me ALL the time about God. They witnessed to me ALL the time, until finally I accepted the Lord in my life in 1980 at seventeen years old. In 1983, I became serious about my relationship with God.

Something within me changed and I felt different. I wanted to do what was right in God's eyes. You probably wonder what a young girl can do that she would need to change. Well young people lie, cheat, and say things they shouldn't. I didn't want to do those things any longer; I saw life through a different lens. I would see worship now and wondered how different was it from praise in terms of feelings? People would bow down, kneel, their cries were different, and their tongues are different. What made them so different I wondered?

Do they have a connection with God that I don't? Are their prayers being answered? Are they going through something? Wanting a changed life, will have you ask questions. Although, I wanted to serve God, I slipped up from time to time. That's right; they say it's only human to mess up sometimes. I even thought having a boyfriend who went to church would keep me on track. Guess what? Even the guys in the church aren't perfect. So, I still had questions.

One day my questions were answered during a trip my church choir took to Baltimore. We sang well that day! My choir mate, Deidre Harper sang the lead for a song entitled, "Holy One." Every single time Deidre sang that song, the power of God would show up so strong. However, this particular time I felt like never before. That was it! The weeping and the feelings of surrender that came over me were indescribable. It was official! I wanted the Lord to be a part of my life wholeheartedly.

I found out that worship is adoration and an intimate relationship with the Father. The closer I got to God, the more my expression toward Him changed. Was it because I needed Him? Absolutely! I got closer to Him because there were things I couldn't do or handle on my own. However, the moment I wasn't concerned about what He could do for me, but was more concerned with giving God what was due Him, I finally understood the word 'Worship' and how it's more than praise. I also understood there was a place closer to God where nothing else mattered. I felt strong, vulnerable, yet comfortable to be myself, all at the same time.

I let go of every pain and issue. Worshipping in public was no problem for me either. In God's presence I felt safe. In those moments, I didn't care what people thought, whereas, I would care in the past.

Once you have an encounter with God, it's beyond description. Worship takes you to a place of love, faith, peace and order. Everything around you takes a back seat to worship; everything that's chaotic settles down; faith goes to another level, and the love of God envelops you. A lot of what I learned about worship was also due to visiting other houses of worship.

My friends and I would leave our service at St. Paul and travel to Pilgrim Church where Bishop Roy Brown was the Pastor. As soon as you walked in that church you'd feel the power of God. I also had the pleasure of meeting a woman named Patricia Rodgers. Pastor Pat had a prayer group called Oil of Joy Ministries, and I'd go with Lynda, or whoever was going. This is also where I'd encounter God. All of this love for God around me, but I still had my issues of wanting God, and wanting to do my thing without consequence.

In 1984, while singing, shouting and worshipping, I was dealing with a church boy and got pregnant. Oh Lord! Back then when you got pregnant out of wedlock you couldn't sing in the choir on Sunday. I had to sit down, but the funny thing is, the guy was able to sing on the choir. Go figure! For a moment I didn't think there was any chance of regaining my place with God. I thought He was upset with me. However, I had a group of people that made sure to encourage me all the time. Deidre Harper, Louise Square, Earl Johnson and Charlotte

Rowe were a blessing. As a matter of fact, every member of the choir loved on me. They admonished me to keep my head up. When we had to sing outside of the church (Earl being the President), let me sing. Oh how I loved singing and did so until the day I gave birth to my son Alonzo Lonell on September 19, 1984.

The love that comes from having a child is unexplainable. At that point, I didn't care who wanted me, I just wanted to take care of my son. I made sure Alonzo was reared in church, that he sung the choir and had a Christian education. He attended Bethlehem Baptist Academy. We did everything together. Yes, when I was in church, he was in church. I even became the director of the children's choir to make sure I was with him during his Christian walk. We were in church a lot, but we had balance in our lives. We'd go to Disney World and small trips to give him time to enjoy his childhood.

I knew there had to be more to my walk with God. There was more for me to do, and in 1995 my cousin Yvette Lemmon heard the voice of God to start her own church called Deliverance Tabernacle. That was one of the happiest days of my life to join her ministry. I knew she loved God, and I was going wherever she went.

The weight of worship became a part of me. Pastor Lemmon saw something in me that I didn't want to see, so much so, that my first sermon preached was "Personal Experience Have You Had Yours Yet." One of the greatest things happened that day. My father, the late Ellis Billings, who didn't attend church, came to hear me preach. Lord Jesus, my father got saved! Listen here! When your worship and surrender before God leads your family to salvation, it is a blessing. Good God all day, my dad continued attending church. He'd even come to video every service we had so he could watch it again at home. My dad loved the way my cousin Yvette preached. He would often say she made it easy to understand the word. Not long after giving his life to Jesus, my dad suddenly passed away. You can imagine that was the worse day of my life. However, I was able to hold it together because I knew my father was saved and learned to love God for himself.

I loved working for my church. I was my Pastor's secretary, and usher and I would also plan the Building Fund church services. One day for our church anniversary I invited my boyfriend to come preach. That's right I started dating a preacher; something I never anticipated. His name was Jonathan Shaw. To me he came out of nowhere. Apparently he saw me, but I never saw him. How did we meet? I ministered in song at an Ordination for Pastor Patricia Rodgers, and he inquired about me to his friend Wesley Wiley. Wesley was the initiator, as he shared that John was interested. From that encounter, it was history. Meeting him was magical, and refreshing. He loved God too. I finally dated someone who loved God, and cared about me. I finally had a person who was close enough to me to teach me more of God. I would watch him preach in awe. I'd talk to myself and say 'How does he know so much?' I found out you can't preach just from experience, you've got to read and being around John, pushed me to learn more.

As I was saying, I invited John to come preach for Deliverance Tabernacles' 2nd year anniversary, and I ushered that day. Out of nowhere, he calls me up to share a prophetic word. John begins to speak the word of the Lord over my life. Mind you we'd just had a conversation the night before about not wanting him to call me out to prophesy to me. I guess this time of sharing was needed. As he began to give me what the Lord said, I began to cry as the word really dealt with me. He closed the word by asking me a question, Would I Marry Him? I was in total shock, but it was the happiest day of my life. Everyone was screaming and shouting all over the church. His parents were even there to record the wonderful moment. I've got to tell you, I honestly thought I'd never get to the place of marriage. I thought it wasn't going to happen for me. But it all turned around. Not only that, after John's proposal, my soon to be mother-in-law and I would take turns praying every day. This really was a confirmation that I was on the right path.

    Now I'm engaged and going with my fiancé wherever he has to preach, including his church. He then attended Beginning A New Life Worship Center. I didn't want to leave my church because I was afraid that I would lose my experience of worship. Honestly I knew that Oil of Joy and Pilgrim Church had worship, and definitely my church Deliverance Tabernacle had worship, but now I had to go somewhere in hopes that I could worship there too. I thought leaving my Deliverance Tabernacle family would leave a void; but it was filled with my fellow worshippers at Beginning Anew. When the presence of God showed up there, I was weak. Now when I say weak I mean I had given God my all and I had nothing left. Pastor Andre

Cook saw me as a worshipper and also pushed me to preach the gospel. Singing was one thing, but preaching is totally different. I never imagined myself preaching on a regular basis, and never desired to do so. But when I did minister the word of God, I wanted to make sure that adoration was toward the Lord. When I sing a song, I worship the Father. When I encountered worship, I entered a place I could go by myself in song.

In 1998 I married my biggest cheerleader Jonathan I. Shaw. Now I lived with a worshipper. We talked about worship and what it meant. We talked about Praise and Worship and what that meant. He would often tell me after I had a God encounter "Sabrina you have to learn not to leave the people." This is funny to me now because my husband would say "You left the people." I would say, huh? He said, "You went into worship without taking the people with you." That was hard for me to comprehend because my response was, "They need to go for themselves." However, I had to remember no one showed me how to get there either. People need to be shown the way.

I promised God, this gift of song He gave me, would only be used to worship Him. Therefore a sense of conviction comes over me when anything else tries to supersede that. Be careful what you use your gift for.

Why did I write this book?
Let's talk about God and Worship and the several things it entails; all of which I've experienced on my quest to finding out the true mean-

ing of worship. I believe there are certain steps you should take before you can get to a place of true worship. I'm not saying that worship will be non-existent if you don't do these things, but I do believe these principles will get you to a place of wholeness. While in worship I believe layers are taken off, and some are put on. Worship is armor! We shouldn't let anything damage our armor or hinder our worship. There are many who question how does one get to a place where worshipping God is a permanent fixture in your life? Here are some tools that have helped me and have been instrumental and inspirational in finding myself in worship. I encourage you to dive in and utilize the note pages to personally evaluate your worship walk. I pray that these tools bless you and draw you even closer in your worship with the Lord.

INNER

But God told Samuel, "Looks aren't everything. Don't be impressed with his looks and stature. I've already eliminated him. GOD judges persons differently than humans do. Men and women look at the face; GOD looks into the heart."
–1 Samuel 16:7 (MSG)

Self-Examination
The Study of One's Behavior and Motivation

Examine yourselves, as to whether you are in faith. Test yourselves.
Do you not know yourselves, that Jesus Christ is in you?
unless indeed you are disqualified. –2 Corinthian 13:5

There's nothing like checking yourself first. It's necessary to do a consistent check of your heart motives behind what you do for the Lord. Our consistent and inner question should be, "God, are You pleased with what You see and know about me?"

In other words, test and evaluate yourself to see whether or not you pass to go to the next level in your relationship with the Father. Again, self-examination is honest self-reflection. Here are a few introspection questions you can use a model:

- Have I moved from being a person that knows of God, to knowing God?
- What are His likes and dislikes about me?
- What have I done to please Him with my walk, my talk, and my life?
- Has anything changed on the inside of me? If so, is my change for the good or bad?
- Am I holding on to my faith?

Although there are many questions to ask yourself, the most important one is, "Do I or others see Jesus in me?" Upon examining yourself, if you don't see Jesus in you, then a greater examination must take place.

I've said to myself, 'listen you shouldn't commune with God without examining yourself.' When I think of communing with God, it's like we're dining together. Can I sit at the table with God and eat with Him knowing there's something not right about me; there's more of something else in me, than Him? Have I done a heart check?

Many people talk about their ability to discern others. However, before we can discern anyone else, we must first discern ourselves. 1 Corinthians 11:28 says, "But let a man examine himself." Some results of non-examination are weakness, illness, and sometimes death. Self-examination will keep us strong and healthy. Why? When you commune with God, you're not just feeding your physical appetite, but your spiritual appetite. Do a self-check and embrace two words... 'under subjection!'

WORSHIPPER THOUGHTS!

Today, I truthfully examine my heart, soul and spirit and see that...

Prayer

A solemn request for help, dialogue, communication between you and God

Be anxious for nothing; but in everything by prayer and supplication with thanksgiving let your requests be made known unto God.
–Philippians 4:6

I hear it all the time, prayer changes things, people and absolutely everything in between. A prayer life is necessary to stay grounded in worship. Create a time and space for communication with the Father; your time to talk and listen. Remember, in prayer God is speaking too.

Oh, but prayer is even more than that. It's a form of acknowledging Him for who He is. In prayer we too express adoration, admiration, frustrations, ask for direction, and seek wisdom. The thing about prayer is, we can pray about all things at all times.

I used to think prayer had a style, but in time I've learned prayer didn't have a certain form. Prayer was unique in that it sounded like your unique self, speaking to a unique God. Your tone, your verbiage; how long or short you prayed didn't matter.

I must admit, I thought only the pastors and leaders could pray. I thought they were the only one God would listen to. In the Catholic Church, there was a place you'd go, a room with a door. When you wanted to speak to God, you had to go through the priest. You would tell the priest about your sin and they would go to God on your behalf. But remember I told you I learned who God was for myself, and all that I wasn't taught, I learned on my own. The biggest lesson I learned was I could go to God for myself. Once that revelation came, I was excited to know that when I prayed, He'd hear me himself.

Did you know that we pray at times, not realizing we are doing it? This is not to diminish anyone's prayer life, but out of nowhere did you ever say "Lord I wish this pain would go away", or "Lord I sure hope I find a parking space." Out of habit you communicated with God through prayer.

Prayer isn't something we do because we need something; prayer keeps our relationship with God fresh and new. It's like a friend you keep in constant contact with to see how they're doing. And when you're not doing so well, you share that intimate part of you only that person can understand. That's the friend who assures you everything will be alright. That's prayer with the Father.

I'd be remiss if I didn't share you may not get what you ask for right away. But don't stop your worship because you think your prayer wasn't given attention. Don't put your praise on pause because you think there's a hiccup in your submission. Pray without ceasing.

WORSHIPPER THOUGHTS!

My prayers for today are?

REPENTANCE

THE ACTION OF REPENTING, WITH SINCERE REGRET OR REMORSE. EACH PERSON WHO TURNS TO GOD IN GENUINE REPENTANCE AND FAITH WILL BE SAVED

I have not come to call the righteous, but sinners, to repentance.
–Luke 5:32

I believe it takes a strong and wise person to admit their faults and turn away from them. To no longer want to repeat the same bad behaviors or sins speaks volumes. Have you turned away from your offenses i.e. sins? Do you know we are all sinners? Those who are guilty should repent. Repentance is when you say to God, 'I am committed to change.' "We all have sinned, and come short." What have we come short to? The glory of and the fullness of God! Repentance is about God's entire presence. And if we don't repent there's no possible way for us to reach that place.

Honestly, there is no perfect person out there. Our human side, the fleshly part of us messes up. Some may say we're all not that bad, but to God's law we fall short. Lack of repentance equals lack of effort to be more like Him!

When I know the presence of the Lord has shown up, I go right into repentance? "Father forgive me," is what I say first because I don't want to worship with dirty hands. It's as though the Lord is standing right there. Everything that's not right within me seems to be magnified. That's right, even me! No one is exempt from repentance as a worshipper.

There's an opportunity of repentance right now, what would you like to tell the Father? A contrite heart He will not despise (Psalm 51).

Worshipper Thoughts!

What do I need to confess?

_____

_____

_____

What do I need to repent for?

_____

_____

_____

What do I need to let go so I can get closer to worship?

_____

_____

_____

HUMILITY

A MODEST OR LOW VIEW OF ONE'S OWN IMPORTANCE; HUMBLENESS.

A man's pride will bring him low,
But the humble in spirit will retain honor. –Proverbs 29:23

God gives grace to the humble. Who doesn't want grace? We can't be arrogant and prideful, and humble at the same time. If seeking to be a true worshipper, humility is the principal and first characteristic to embrace. Remember it's not about you, it's about our Lord and Savior Jesus Christ. People would love to take the credit for a lot of things they shouldn't. When you constantly put words like 'I did' in front of tasks, that's not humble. No one is perfect!

What I've found is people are drawn to others who reveal their true self in a lowly view. Most think that's a safe place. When you're humble you don't use your position to get where you want to be. You support and promote others, rather than promote yourself.

Let nothing be done through selfish ambition or conceit,
but in lowliness of mind let each esteem others better than himself.
–Philippians 2:3-4

A wise man is humble. Never mistake that a humble person has low-self esteem and doesn't stand up for themselves. The more a man is humble before God, the more he is exalted. Humility is not fleshly. Flesh and humility do not mix. Humility comes from God.

In the Bible we know that David showed humility first when he was chosen out of all his brothers to be the next King. He went back to working in the field without letting what just happened or what he was told go to his head. David served who he was to replace with all humility. Whatever he was told to do, he did gracefully. David had ample opportunity to kill Saul, but he waited patiently for his turn to be who God had called him to be long ago.

There is a young man that attends our church Crown Ministries International, Inc. and he serves as a Deacon. His name is Rory Ramos. Not only is he a 'worshipper,' but he is one of the most humble men I know. Deacon Rory, who recently married, was hit with a family situation of his wife becoming ill less than a year of being married. Deacon Rory put any and everything before himself. It's as though he had no concern for himself, but all concern for his wife and those around him. He still finds time to come to the church to pray, clean and fellowship. He works with troubled youth, goes home to care for his healed wife, and takes care of himself later. If you want to see the epitome of humility just look at Rory Ramos or someone in your proximity that has similar attributes of serving God and family.

WORSHIPPER THOUGHTS!

Am I humble?

___

___

___

Do I feel the need to boast?

___

___

___

Do I put others before me?

___

___

___

Do I enjoy making others happy?
_____
_____
_____

Do I believe people or life owes me something?
_____
_____
_____

FORGIVENESS

THE ACTION OR PROCESS OF FORGIVING OR BEING FORGIVEN

*Let the redeemed of the Lord say so, whom
He has redeemed from the hand of the enemy. –Psalm 107:2*

Forgiveness is an act of worship. Forgiveness also frees you to worship. If we don't possess a forgiving heart how can we stand before God? It's an act of love, mercy and grace.

Jesus was the perfect example of forgiveness and worship as He hung on the cross. Hanging between two thieves, He is asked by one to remember him when He gets to paradise, Jesus does just that. If He can forgive those who persecuted Him, He will forgive you too (Luke 23:34). In forgiveness, there is also reconciliation. We should do our best to seek it daily. We often hear the saying, "forgiveness is not just you asking forgiveness from God, but from others." The saying is true. Many people would like to limit forgiveness to just asking the Lord. We say things, and before you know it, it has been released and we can't take it back. If this has happened, consider that when asking for forgiveness, reconciliation may need to take place.

Many of us have heard the familiar story of the prodigal son (Luke 15:11-32). There was a man with two sons. The younger of the two asked for his inheritance before time, and his father granted his request. He was wasteful, extravagant, and spent what he had until there was nothing left. He found himself eating pig slop to fill his belly. He realized that he didn't have to live in that state and returned home willing to be a servant. He knew, at least, the servants at his father's home were eating better than him. Not knowing what to expect when he arrived, his father gave him a reception that was unexpected. Before he made it to where his father was, his dad came to meet him and kissed him. His father told his older brother to bring his robe and ring to place it on his son; he was just glad to have his son home.

Sometimes we miss out because we think the people we hurt won't or don't forgive us. Forgiveness isn't something you wear on the outside, it's internal. Mark 11:25. "And whenever you stand praying, if you have anything against anyone, forgive him, that your Father in heaven may also forgive you your trespasses

Worshipper Thoughts!

What do I need to ask God to forgive?

_____

_____

_____

Who do I need to forgive?

_____

_____

_____

Who needs to forgive me?

_____

_____

_____

Do I need to reconcile with someone?
___
___
___

INTIMACY
CLOSE FAMILIARITY OR FRIENDSHIP

*He who has My commandments and keeps them, it is he who loves Me.
And he who loves Me will be loved by My Father, and I will love him and
manifest Myself to him. –John 14:21*

I thought knowing of God was good enough. However, when I became more acquainted, the intimacy became more personal. I wanted to know about Him. I know the saying "He may not come when you want Him, but He's right on time." When He is with you, it feels like He never misses a beat. That's how my moments of intimacy with God are.

There are things that I honestly don't share with anyone else other than God during my intimate times with Him. It's as if there's an audience of one. I really feel like God knows me. It's the experience of being very close. Little children have their imaginary friend that no one else can see but them, but we have Jesus. You may think that's a bad analogy, but it's mine. The Lord is someone in who I can relate and seems to always understand.

It's amazing to know you can be close to someone. Although you feel their presence, they're far away. Now most people who are intimate know who they are intimate with. So there are some things you should know about God to be intimate with Him. How can you worship someone you don't know? If you don't know anything, know this, He's a jealous God. Once you're intimate with Him, another god won't do! The Lord should be able to trust that you won't step out of the relationship. When you trust someone, you allow them to get close to you. The closer you are to me, or the closer I allow you in my space, the more I trust you.

It wasn't until Hannah became intimate with the Father that her petition was granted. Yes she prayed every year when she went to the temple. It was when she understood that something different within her had to take place, that she received the answer for her request. Even Eli noticed something different about her. She finally got in the face of God, and allowed him to take full control. Her intimacy released her womb from bareness to fruitful (Samuel 1:2-2:21).

Worshipper Thoughts!

Am I intimate enough with God?

_____

_____

_____

Do I trust God with the intimate parts of me?

_____

_____

_____

Do I set aside enough time for Him and me alone?

_____

_____

_____

Am I learning more of God?

_____

_____

_____

Am I worshipping anything else more than Him?

_____

_____

_____

HEALING

THE PROCESS OF MAKING OR
BECOMING SOUND OR HEALTHY AGAIN

He heals the brokenhearted and binds up their wounds. –Psalm 147:3

I haven't personally been sick unto death, but I do thank God for all healing He's done for me and those connected to me. Have you ever been in worship when you didn't feel well and God healed your body? I've seen God add years to someone's life because of their worship.

We all know that God's power is not limited to physical healing. He has no limits or boundaries. Mental illness and emotional healing are just a few things. The word of God says "Let everything that has breath praise the Lord!" So don't think those who have issues of the mind can't worship. The scripture says in Mark 5:5 "Day and night a man was in the tombs, crying and cutting himself with stones. But when he saw Jesus afar off, he ran and worshipped." This man had breath in his body and a mental issue, but still knew to worship. What does that say about us? For some of us it says, we will allow our depression and state of affect, to effect our worship to God.

True story! I have a close knit, immediate family and I also married into one. Not long after meeting my in-laws Rudolph and

Gwenda Shaw, she shared a story of her and my father in-love being in a car accident with two other friends while traveling south on the highway. Daddy Shaw was driving and fell asleep behind the wheel. She was nine months pregnant with my husband John. The car flipped over several times and she was the only one not injured. Gwenda also told me prior to that, also while carrying my husband, she was diagnosed with Cervical Cancer. Encouraged to abort my husband, she was and is a prayer warrior. She believed that God would heal, and God certainly did.

Another miracle of healing she shared with me concerned my sister-in-love Yolanda Shaw. Yolanda was born deaf, blind and with heart problems. While Gwenda was carrying Yolanda, she contracted German Measles. At two-years-old Yolanda had to have heart surgery. As a matter of fact, she had several surgeries. The doctor's only gave Yolanda a few years to live. I already told you Mother Shaw was a prayer warrior, and she totally trusts God. One night she put her trust in action by throwing Yolanda's medicines' in the garbage. Her prayer was "Lord if you want her to live, let her live, if not, take her." Three days went by, ten years went by, and Yolanda lived until she was 44 years-old. God is a healer. Is there an illness or issue you want healing from?

WORSHIPPER THOUGHTS!

What do I need healing from?

_____

_____

_____

What is the first step I need to take toward healing?

_____

_____

_____

Do I trust God to heal?

_____

_____

_____

Is my lack of healing affecting my worship?
___
___
___

FEARLESSNESS
THE LACK OF FEAR

Say to those who are fearful-hearted, "Be strong, do not fear!
Behold, your God will come with vengeance,
With the recompense of God; He will come and save you." –Isaiah 35:4

How often have we heard "If you're going to pray don't worry, but if you're going to worry don't pray? You must be fearless when you pray and not worry about anything. There's a boldness that comes with fearlessness. There's a confidence in also believing.

There's nothing like being on your own with a child. I became a single mother at 21 years-old. Being the person I was, I didn't want my parents to take care of me so I got a job and saved money until I could move out. As much as I wanted to be on my own, it was scary. I was afraid I wouldn't be able to do it. How in the world could I provide for me and my son; keep food on the table, clothes on our backs, and put him through private school? There were people around who discouraged walking in fear and reminded me that God had me. I heard all of that, but I couldn't receive it when I didn't have enough. When I couldn't wash clothes, fix a meal for my son, and had to tell a lie Con Edison is fixing the lights, it was stressful. If I didn't have a relationship with God, I would have never believed them or myself for that matter.

I had to learn quickly, there is no time to allow my fear to captivate me to a point where I'm helpless. I had to remind myself; God formed me so He got me!

When you're fearless you must be confident in who you are and what you believe. Isaiah 43:1-2a But now, says the Lord, who created you, O Jacob, And He who formed you, O Israel: Fear not, for I have redeemed you; I have called you by your name: You are mine. When you pass through the waters, I will be with you..."

The daughters of Zelophehad changed the culture of their day. After the death of their father, these five sisters fearlessly got together to request their inheritance. Zelophehad had no sons, and usually the sons were the next in line. Because they spoke up, and had no fear they expanded the legal rights of women during that time (Numbers 27).

Abigail was married to Nabal, a very stubborn and harsh man. Nabal had choice words for David when David requested payment for looking out for Nabal's flock. Word came to Abigail that Nabal's mouth got him in trouble, and that David was on his way to collect payment himself. Nabal's men tell Abigail and immediately she prepares her horse with items to head David off. Without fear and not knowing what would happen to her, Abigail jumped into action. Abigail was fearless, as she began to tell David who he was in God. She was also quick on her feet (1Samuel 25).

Fear is not of God!

WORSHIPPER THOUGHTS!

What are some of my biggest fears?

_____

_____

_____

_____

_____

_____

How can I quench my get rid of my fears through worship?

_____

_____

_____

_____

_____

_____

FOCUSED

THE CENTER OF INTEREST OR ACTIVITY

*Let your eyes look straight ahead,
And your eyelids look right before you. –Proverbs 4:25*

In living a life of worship, there is a constant question we must ask ourselves. Is the Lord the center of my interest?

Often we get off focus in worship when trying to meet the Lord. Finding out where He is becomes a task. Think about it! Even while you're worshipping, if something is going on around you, do you stop your worship to see what was going on?

How about this one, while in worship you thought about all you had to do? It was at that time that everything else seemed to captivate your attention. Something dropping on the floor, a baby crying, others demanding our time and everything else screamed louder than your moment of worship. You just couldn't focus. Once you allow other things to take precedence, those things become your god.

How can we be in the presence of God and lose sight of him? I'll tell you how! The focus wasn't there initially. There was a thought of worship, but the act of worship gives way to present reality. This means, we weren't focused on worship in the first place. If a sound that doesn't sound like God can get us out of the presence or away from an audience with him, then it's not worship. It entertainment!

Don't allow anything to drown out your cry to God. Don't let your worship take a back seat to what can wait. What's getting your attention? Even our phones are equipped to tell someone we are focused on driving and what they need must wait. This invention was created so that we can remain focused on what's around us. If you stay focused, all those other things will work out.

A perfect example of a distraction when worship was present and needed was in a moment with Mary and Martha. We know they loved Jesus, but when Jesus came to their house all Martha wanted to do was serve. Mind you her service to Jesus was a form of worship. It's just her worship was different then everyone else. Now you would think there's nothing wrong with her serving; somebody had to do it. And take into consideration that it's Martha's house.

Many people would have a problem with Martha's reaction to Mary not helping her as she prepared for Jesus. And to add insult to injury, when Martha tries to get Jesus to agree with her; Jesus gives Martha an answer she didn't expect. Jesus tells Martha that Mary has chosen the better part.

Jesus says Mary chose to focus on Me and not the doings of things. Mary has chosen to worship. Mary has chosen to spend time with Me. Hmm, I mean Jesus is in the house. He is touchable; you can actually see Him. While Martha is trying to find Mary, Mary is at the feet of Jesus. Now was Martha mad because Mary was at Jesus' feet, or was she mad that she herself wasn't at Jesus' feet because she had things to do? For a moment Martha thought what she was doing was more important than focusing on Jesus being there. She was focused alright, but on the wrong thing. Too often when Jesus shows up, we are idolizing other parts of our life. When He's there, give Him all your attention.

The enemy would love for us to focus on, our rent, our health, everyday life issues, and not focus on the one who can handle all these issues. The woman who built the prophet Elisha a room in her house didn't have a special need, but it was seen that she didn't have a child. The Lord blessed her womb. The Focus, the #1 blessing is, regardless of what she didn't have, she still didn't lose sight of what she could do for the man of God. After having the child, the child dies. Focus #2 blessing is, instead of getting upset and turning this horrible problem into a ought against the one who she believed was the reason for the child coming into the world; she gives her situation back to the gift giver of life.

There are many situations in our life that the enemy would love us to halt our worship for, but don't lose focus. Romans 8:5 – For those who live according to the flesh set their minds on the things of the flesh, but those who live according to the Spirit, the things of the Spirit.

Worshipper Thoughts!

Am I focused on or distracted from God's presence?

_____

_____

_____

_____

_____

What can I do to return my focus to God?

_____

_____

_____

_____

_____

TRUTH

THE QUALITY OR STATE OF BEING TRUE

But the hour is coming, and now is, when the true worshipers will worship the Father in spirit and truth; for the Father is seeking such to worship Him. –John 4:23-24

Telling the truth and honesty go hand in hand. We must be honest with ourselves before we can be honest with God. Truth is a matter of the heart! Is your heart one of truth? What is your truth about God? What is the truth about yourself? Can you worship God when the truth of your circumstances are staring you in the face? Remember, God is worthy of all glory and honor no matter how we feel.

We worship in spirit and in truth. According to the word, we do this at the same time. You don't worship in spirit and then truth. Truth is another form of worship.

WORSHIPPER THOUGHTS!

Am I a truthful person?
_____
_____
_____

Have I ever lied?
_____
_____
_____

Have I ever shoplifted?
_____
_____
_____

Have I ever snuck in somewhere without paying?

_____
_____
_____

Are my heart and spirit in alignment with truth?

_____
_____
_____

Do I want truth to reign in my life?

_____
_____
_____

BELIEF

AN ACCEPTANCE THAT A STATEMENT IS TRUE OR THAT SOMETHING EXISTS

For this reason we also thank God without ceasing, because when you received the word of God which you heard from us, you welcomed it not as the word of men, but as it is in truth, the word of God, which also effectively works in you who believe. –1Thessalonians 2:13

Belief is to accept what you know to be true. You trust it, and have faith in what you know with confidence.

Many wonder how one can believe in a God not seen. One thing I don't do is argue with people about their belief. I believe that no man could have created the heaven and the earth on his own accord. My belief is that God put the stars and the moon in the sky. My God also created the seas and sand. I also believe that He's Lord of all. You shouldn't have faith in anyone or anything you don't trust or believe.

My belief is Monotheism; that is I believe in One God; Jehovah. I'd rather believe God does exist, and find out that He doesn't, than to not believe He exists and find out He does.

I believe God loves me more than anything in this world. I'm not perfect. Everyday, I'm grateful God allows me to see another day. In my daily walk, I see the mercies of God on my life. When I could have been elsewhere doing something other than being a wife, mother and Pastor, it amazes me. You can't tell me not to believe God for who He is.

Many don't believe in something unless they can see it and want tangible results of their belief. People will believe there is a god, but not believe in God, because they can't see or touch Him.

I don't need all of that. I believe Jesus was born from the Virgin Mary, was crucified, died and was buried, and is coming back for me. I believe God.

WORSHIPPER THOUGHTS!

What do I believe about God?

___

___

___

Do I truly believe He died for my sins?

___

___

___

Do I believe in His power at convenient times or all the time?

___

___

___

UNCONDITIONAL LOVE
TO LOVE WITHOUT LIMITATIONS

The LORD has appeared [a]of old to me, saying:
Yes, I have loved you with an everlasting love;
Therefore with lovingkindness I have drawn you. –Jeremiah 31:3

God chose to love us unconditionally before the world was formed. He loves us despite what He forsees in us and before we meet any criteria. Isn't that an awesome fact to know? Can you imagine what God's love for us looks or feels like when we worship Him? Oh my goodness!

I get excited knowing when others say they love me but God's love is without condition. There's no, I'll love you if you love me or strings attached. I don't have to give God anything for Him to love me unconditionally. When I worship, I find myself loving God unconditionally. It's not about what He'll give me when I'm done; it's about what I give Him in that moment.

How many can say they love someone without knowing where they came from or what they've done? Often I've heard people give the following analogy and question when you meet someone. Does the person they just met start at 100 in your eyes, or do they start at 0 and work themselves up to 100? How do you see an individual that you don't know? Can you love them without any reservations? I believe true worshippers love without condition of one's past. 1 Corinthians 16:14 "Let all that you do be done with love."

WORSHIPPER THOUGHTS!

How can I follow Christ's example of unconditional love?
_____
_____
_____

Can I tell the difference between conditional and unconditional love?
_____
_____
_____

Can I love someone when it looks like they don't love me back?
_____
_____
_____

Do I love my children unconditionally? How?
_____
_____
_____

Do I love God but hate my brother or sister?
_____
_____
_____

OUTER

Here's another way to put it: You're here to be light, bringing out the God-colors in the world. God is not a secret to be kept. We're going public with this, as public as a city on a hill. If I make you light-bearers, you don't think I'm going to hide you under a bucket, do you? I'm putting you on a light stand. Now that I've put you there on a hilltop, on a light stand – shine! Keep open house; be generous with your lives. By opening up to others, you'll prompt people to open up with God, this generous Father in heaven.
–Matthew 5:14-16 (MSG)

BEING AN EXAMPLE
A THING CHARACTERISTIC OF ITS KIND
OR ILLUSTRATING A GENERAL RULE

Let your light so shine before men, that they may
see your good works, and glorify your Father in heaven. –Matthew 5:16

I once preached a message entitled "Turn on your light, so we don't trip." Many people are tripping over so called believers, because they aren't shedding any light on themselves. What do I mean? When people can't tell the difference between a believer and an unbeliever, they're liable to trip and get caught up in the same things because there is no example. If I see a life of integrity, humility, conviction and worship, the visual would help me in my struggle and want to do what's right in God's eyes.

We brothers and sisters, my fellow worshippers are the salt of the earth. Our job is to add the flavor of God on this earth so men would want to taste and see that the Lord He is good. We cannot think we can live away from a world that contradicts what we as, confessors of Christ, believe. In other words you can't live on this earth in isolation. It's bad enough when we get in our churches on a Sunday morning the things around us are far from us. As examples we are called to a responsibility. That responsibility is not just for Apostles, Bishops,

Pastors, or Ministers, but all who are holy are the salt of the earth, examples – and we are to season others.

Salt preserves, salt adds flavor, and without it, there is a bland taste. We need to help those who are living a bland life. An example I used in my message, was that if meat (the world) went bad, it's not the meats fault; it is the lack of preservatives (the salt) that did not do its job.

In your worship to God, you should be the flavor to someone's life. Be the example they need for preservation on this earth. Salt produces thirst, so I guess salt is good in that aspect. If you're living for Christ in front of someone the way He expects, it should make others thirsty to know Christ and drink the living water so they will never thirst again. As a believer, we must be cognizant that we are an example to different people at different times.

To my children, I strive to be the greatest example of a mother/worshipper they will ever see. A person should never be one example at home but another in public. Children will see you in your purest form. For me, I'll worship God at home and in His temple. Worship is not for show, it's so God will be glorified.

My extended family needs to know Jesus, and the life I live in front of them at family gatherings, holiday's, or whenever, should never be compromised. If anyone needs to see the life I live to get closer to Jesus its my extended family.

On my previous job, my coworkers had much respect for me. It wasn't a secret I was saved and loved God. I took time out of my day on occasion to pray. I took God with me to work every single day. God made a way for me to have that job. Allow people to know the God you serve; don't keep Him to yourself.

At Crown Ministries I must be an example of worship. How do you get people to follow you if you're a non-worshipper? It may look like external worship, but real worship can be seen internally.

WORSHIPPER THOUGHTS!

Am I the salt of the earth?

_____

_____

_____

Do I live two lives?

_____

_____

_____

Am I an example of Christ to my family, work and church?

_____

_____

_____

SONG OF THE LORD
SONG DEVELOPED BY BEING IN THE PRESENCE OF THE LORD

*My lips shall greatly rejoice when I sing unto to you,
And my soul, which You have redeemed. –Psalm 71:23*

A Hymn is a type of song, usually religious, specifically written for the purpose of adoration or prayer, and typically addressed to a deity or deities, or a prominent figure or personification. The word hymn derives from the Greek word hymnos, which means song of praise.

The Song of the Lord is not a common phrase. If you ask some people they can't tell you what that statement means.

The song of the Lord for me is when the Holy Spirit gives a song not written, but comes from within. It's a song to God, about God. I've found the Song of the Lord, gets a person to a place where a normal song can't. Now when I say normal, that doesn't mean the songs we hear aren't wonderful, they truly are. But the song of the Lord is impromptu inspired. It's what God is doing at the moment to impact, deliver and set free those in the atmosphere of worship.

Most of the time, the song of the Lord isn't a song you will sing every Sunday. When inspired, it was to the Lord at that time, for that time and assists in taking worship to another level.

I've known the song of the Lord to be started by one person, but others join in. You don't have to be a singer to be inspired with the song of the Lord. Church service is not the only place this action can drop in your spirit, but the privacy in your home works as well.

Create an atmosphere where the song of the Lord can be created. Psalm 149:1 – Praise the Lord. Sing unto the Lord a new song, and his praise in the assembly of saints.

WORSHIPPER THOUGHTS!

How can I integrate more Hymns in my worship?

_____

_____

_____

In devotion, do I allow the Holy Spirit to flow through song?

_____

_____

_____

Do I actively participate in praise and worship at church?

_____

_____

_____

READING THE WORD

TO LOOK AT AND COMPREHEND THE MEANING OF WRITTEN OR PRINTED MATTER

Be diligent to present yourself approved to God, a worker who does not need to be ashamed, rightly dividing the word of truth.
–2 Timothy 2:15

I admit this was a challenge for me. It's not that I don't love the word, but my biggest issue was understanding. The greatest help I've found is the different versions and translations; my favorite being the Message Bible. Don't let your lack of understanding the word be a hindrance. It's important to learn how to digest the word so it can nourish and bring life to you.

Familiarize, get acquainted and guard yourself against misapplying the word of God. In other words be diligent in your studying so you can handle the word accurately. Hold a personal Bible study. I don't mean host one in your house, although it can be done. But study your Bible for self-understanding. Invest in your life.

Unfortunately, there are many who will misuse God's word for their own gain. If we don't study, we will find ourselves believing everything. Not only that, one's interpretation of the word can be different than your own. The word clearly states, the lack of knowledge will have you to perish.

Worshipper Thoughts!

Am I writing notes and scriptures when I hear the sermon on Sunday?

_____

_____

_____

Am I reading the word to understand?

_____

_____

_____

Am I setting aside enough time for personal Bible study?

_____

_____

_____

Am I applying the word to my life correctly or for selfish gain?
___
___
___

PATIENCE

THE CAPACITY TO ACCEPT OR TOLERATE DELAY, TROUBLE OR SUFFERING WITHOUT GETTING ANGRY OR UPSET

Now may the God of patience and comfort grant you to be likeminded toward one another according to Christ Jesus. –Romans 15:5

Patience is one thing I never wanted to pray for. I've heard so many stories about asking for patience. Many say when you pray for patience, you are tested. I've been told it's the worse experience ever and nothing you want or desire will come fast enough. If you pray for patience you won't be happy with the results.

Wait, isn't patience one of the first things Paul speaks of when he talks about love in Galatians; Love is patient and teaches you to wait, just like God waits on us.

I must admit, without asking for patience, I believe God has tried to teach me how to deal in this area. Many things have tested me throughout the years. I remember when I wanted a child so bad after getting married. Every month I waited with anticipation my desire to have another child would happen. Every month for two years I felt disappointment. All I kept hearing was be patient. I heard it so much I started to hate the word Patience. I didn't understand why it was taking so long. Then one day I said to myself, let me try this thing called patience. Maybe if I stop thinking about it and hounding God about bringing my dream to fruition, it will work out. After a while, I didn't even think about it every month, and before I knew it, I was pregnant.

Recently I've been tested again with patience. Please don't judge what I'm about to say, but I felt like I had to learn all over again. My mother came to live with me and my family. Since she is now 91 years old, she requires around the clock care. It's a challenge when our parents are set in their ways and want things the way they want them. It's hard to see the woman who reared you, and took care of you, getting older and unable to care for herself. There are moments when she will remember things from years ago but can't remember what she ate yesterday. One day she could walk, and now she needs assistance. I'm caring for the woman who, in my eyes, is the strongest woman I've ever known. I've had to come to grips with her getting older and all she needs while she's with me, I must supply. I've had to be patient with doing for my mother, just like I did for my babies. Patience can be trying, will bring discomfort, and you may even lose your temper. But when you embrace patience, the reward is great.

Worshipper Thoughts!

Am I inpatient?

_____

_____

_____

Do I need more patience?

_____

_____

_____

In what areas do I need patience?

_____

_____

_____

TIME

THE INDEFINITE CONTINUED PROGRESS OF EXISTENCE AND EVENTS IN THE PAST, PRESENT, AND FUTURE REGARDED AS A WHOLE

But you, when you pray, go into your room, and when you have shut your door, pray to your Father who is in the secret place; and your Father who sees in secret will reward you openly. –Matthew 6:6

Time is precious. It's something we all wish we had more of, but don't use it wisely. Every day we start out creating an agenda; a day that will begin with, or without us. But it's what we do with that time that's important. John 9:4 – I must work the works of him that sent me, while it is day; the night is coming, when no man can work.

How much time will you devote to your family, job, or something or someone else? How much time will you devote to yourself? Better yet, how much time is allotted for God?

The truth is, we can spend time doing so much for others and neglect time with God. So many give explanations that time got away from them. However, the burning questions is, did time get away or was it poor planning?

At the beginning of this book, I shared my experience of worship in my car. It doesn't matter where you are, or what you're doing, you can find time for worship. Do I have a witness? When you think about how wonderful God has been to you and how He takes time to be a blessing; that alone should activate time for worship. God always has time for us.

Make spending time a habit like everything else. Put God on your schedule. Who's in a relationship with someone you don't spend time with? What time do you get to church? There's so much to be missed when we are late. Jesus shows up at 10:00 a.m., but you get there at 11:00 a.m. looking for an encounter that happened already. I know your time is important, but so is the Father's.

Worshipper Thoughts!

Do I put people, places and things before God?

___

Do I make enough time for God?

___

Consistency

Conformity in the Application of Something

For I am the LORD, I do not change;
Therefore you are not consumed, O sons of Jacob. –Malachi 3:6

It's a good thing God is consistent with His love for us. He's a God that doesn't change. He doesn't conform himself to fit certain situations around us. He's the same today, yesterday and forever more.

Consistency can be hard naturally as well as spiritually. It can be difficult to have any kind of consistency when so many things are changing. Even though there is room for change, we must try to incorporate the change to maintain consistency.

No matter what tries to block you from worship, remain consistent in getting it done. In other words, there's an attitude you must take to remain consistent. Inconsistency is of the devil. The enemy wants us believers to be inconsistent in our walk, talk, prayer life, and worship. Some of us are up early and intimate with God on a regular basis, but as soon as something happens with our schedule, one day of no worship turns into two. Don't let anything throw you off in your flow with God. Consistency is habit forming and chaos has not place. Ongoing worship is a must. No matter how many times you may stop, get back to a consistent life of worship. Psalm 89:34 – My covenant will I not break, nor alter the thing that is gone out of my lips.

WORSHIPPER THOUGHTS!

Am I consistent in my worship with God?

_____
_____
_____
_____
_____
_____

The one thing I'm consistent in is?

_____
_____
_____
_____
_____
_____

BALANCE

AN EVEN DISTRIBUTION IF WEIGHT ENABLING SOMEONE OR SOMETHING TO REMAIN UPRIGHT AND STEADY

To everything there is a season,
and a time to every purpose under the heaven:
A time to be born, and a time to die;
a time to plant, and a time to pluck up that which is planted;
A time to kill, and a time to heal;
a time to break down, and a time to build up;
A time to weep, and a time to laugh;
a time to mourn, and a time to dance;
A time to cast away stones, and a time to gather stones together;
a time to embrace and a time to refrain from embracing;
A time to get and a time to lose;
a time to keep, and a time to cast away;
A time to reap, and a time to sew;
a time to keep silence, and a time to speak;
A time to love, and a time to hate;
a time of war, and a time peace.
–Ecclesiastes 3:1–8

Some may want to argue this point, but I believe in balance. Who says you can't be a worshipper and enjoy life? I didn't say live like the world, I said enjoy life. Am I not a lover of God and a worshipper if I go to the movies, or roller-skating, or swimming? No, I am a worshipper with Balance.

I love spending time with God; it's one of my favorite things to do. But to say that I want to be in church all the time, the answer is no. God doesn't mind if you take time to rest your body, read a book, go out to dinner and spend time with your family.

My family is very busy. My husband preaches, teaches, counsels, and runs his businesses. My children all have their own schedule, and I do the chores, take care of my mother, preach and sing. Everyone has a lot on their plate. But we find time to have balance. Listen, we love good church, we can do it all day and night. But you need to take a pause and smell the roses. Sometimes life can be overwhelming and the best way to catch your breath is to step back from the hustle and bustle and take care of you.

The Shaw's try their best to go away at least once or twice a year. Cruises are our thing. When we go on a cruise, we actually don't spend all of our time reading our word. And there are no church services on the ship, so to the shows we go. Do you think we're not worshippers? Trust me; we are worshippers to the core. God gets all the glory no matter what we are doing, or where we are.

Most people will say they don't have time for balance. Well you need to find time. If not, you'll blame God for something He didn't do to you.

WORSHIPPER THOUGHTS!

When was the last time I took some time for me?

_____

_____

_____

When was the last time I had some godly fun?

_____

_____

_____

Do I encourage my family gatherings to have fun?

_____

_____

_____

Do I live a life of balance?

FAMILY

A GROUP CONSISTING OF PARENTS AND CHILDREN; ALL THE DESCENDANTS OF A COMMON ANCESTOR

But if anyone does not provide for his own, and especially for those of his household, he has denied the faith, and is worse than an unbeliever.
–1 Timothy 5:8

Family came in the beginning.

As long as I can remember, I've been a part of a close knit family. The Lord blessed my parents to have 50 years of marriage. I can remember my siblings gathering in my parents room on Sunday morning with our plates to eat breakfast and watch T.V. Can you imagine at least five people in one bed? Those were some fun times. The only other time we would gather like that was for Thanksgiving. Relatives would come over and we'd all gather in the living room with extra chairs eating, talking and laughing.

I've always said "when I have a family, I'm going to enjoy having fun." This came true for me. I have family of my own and we have the best of times. Talk about the laughs we have, the great food, fun and fellowship. There's always a story that comes across the table that I never heard of before. I absolutely love my family. Not only do I have a great family, I married into one. In some ways they are very similar, and in others different, but all the same they are my family.

My husband makes sure that the church doesn't come between him and the family. But the saying is true "A family that prays together stays together."

WORSHIPPER THOUGHTS!

Do I spend enough time with my family?

_____

_____

_____

Do I pray enough for my family?

_____

_____

_____

Are 'things' more important than my family?

_____

_____

_____

MARRIAGE

THE LEGALLY OR FORMALLY RECOGNIZED UNION OF TWO PEOPLE AS PARTNERS IN A PERSONAL RELATIONSHIP

*Two are better than one; Because they have
a good reward for their labor. –Ecclesiastes 4:9*

Marriage is important to God and he wants marriage to reflect His image. If married, ask yourself, does your marriage reflect God's image. What exactly does your marriage look like? Does your marriage look like worship, or do you worship marriage? Do you and your husband worship together? Worship makes marriage more beautiful with time. If you're not married, I pray that you follow these principles in your future.

What I truly love about my union is that I'm married to someone who loves God wholeheartedly. Although married to me, the woman he loves, his worship isn't hindered.

John doesn't have to look at me, neither I him to see if we're in worship before either of us worship. We understand that our worship as a married couple is still separate. To make this a little more clearer, we can worship God at separate times. His worship time may not be mine. This doesn't mean that either of us loves God less because one is worshipping and the other isn't at that particular time. Whatever you do, don't get caught up in worshipping your mate more than God.

We can get lost in loving our spouses to the point of idolizing them. I believe I've crossed this threshold a few times. Please don't judge that statement. I was so happy to finally have someone that loved me for me, I put my husband on a pedestal and no one could knock him off. And you know who taught me not to do that? My husband! He continued to quote the scripture, "Man will fail you, but God never fails." I thought, what do you mean you'll fail me. Talk about taking words literally. But I got it, he's not perfect. He could try his best, give his all, but sometimes the results will be disappointing. Although I believe my husband is the greatest at whatever he does, he still can't do for me what God can. We put so much pressure on our spouses to perform duties that only God can do. Actually, let's go here, there are some things our spouses can do, but that's only with God's assistance.

WORSHIPPER THOUGHTS!

Is family important to me?

_____

_____

_____

Am I an advocate for family?

_____

_____

_____

Do I pray for my family?

_____

_____

_____

Am I idolizing any family members or my spouse?
___
___
___

FUN

ENJOYMENT, AMUSEMENT, OR LIGHTHEARTED PLEASURE

*And also that every man should eat and drink
and enjoy the good of all his labor, it is the gift of God.
–Ecclesiastes 3:13*

God wants us to have a good time. Have fun in our worship. Laugh, socialize, and get the most we can out of life. Laughter is good for you. Smile and give your face a break.

Go to dinner with friends. My friends and I make it a point to go out every so often to catch up. We all love God, but our conversations aren't specifically focused on Him. We do however, talk about our families, work and things around us that God has blessed us to have. So I guess worship to God can always be present.

Some may disagree with this, but there are movies that you can watch. Get a group of friends, family and acquaintances together and go to the movies.

Crown Ministries' One Heart Couples Ministry went hosted outings with other couples. It was a wonderful fellowship. In no way do I believe God was offended by us gathering together, as our respect and love for God was not compromised in any way.

Go on vacation. I know most say, they either don't have time or money for a vacation. All vacations aren't expensive. When my husband and I first got married we had no money for our one year anniversary. We decided to have a mini home vacation in our living room. No one home but us, and had a picnic in the middle of the floor. When you are able to go away, do so. Get your passport and go to an island you've never been before. If you feel guilt when you get there, find a space of solitude; worship God, and then go swimming.

Worshippers have fun too.

WORSHIPPER THOUGHTS!

Am I having fun in life?

ENCOURAGEMENT
THE ACT OF GIVING SOMEONE SUPPORT, CONFIDENCE AND HOPE

Be strong and of good courage, fear not, nor be afraid of them:
for the Lord thy God, He is the one who goes with you.
He will not leave you nor forsake you. –Deuteronomy 31:6

We believers must encourage one another. Sometimes speaking a word of encouragement will bring someone out of a state of depression. Speak life and not death. People just want to know that everything will be alright, and sometimes it matters who shares those words that will bring light to a dark place.

Encouragement should be spoken with authority. Not in the force of it, with tone, but spoken with confidence. The person receiving the encouragement should feel there is hope after their challenge and will be ok.

There are sinners who are waiting to be encouraged. Possibly some of them were previous lovers of God. However, due to the lack of encouragement in the church, they left. Encouragement goes a long way. Now I'm not saying to encourage sin, but encourage them out of where they are. Encouragement should be used to build people up, so that we all can benefit the beauty of God in worship.

Have you ever seen someone in worship and you can tell that brother or that sister needs to be encouraged? You can tell that the form of worship they are giving God in that moment is one of desperation. That is your moment to be used of God to build them up in Jesus. In other words "Bear one another's burdens, and so fulfill the law of Christ."

Once you have encouraged someone else, encourage yourself. How do you encourage yourself? With the word of God! With the Song of the Lord! Let God pour His encouragement into you through His love and His word.

Be encouraged with these scriptures...

Isaiah 41:10 – Fear not, for I am with you; be not dismayed for I am your God; I will strengthen you, Yes, I will help you, I will uphold you with my righteous right hand.

Deuteronomy 31:6 – Be strong and of good courage. Do not fear nor be afraid of them; for the Lord your God, He is the One who goes with you. He will not leave you nor forsake you.

1 Corinthians 10:13 – No temptation has overtaken you except such as is common to man; but God is faithful, who will not allow you to be tempted beyond what you are able, but with the temptation will also make the way of escape, that you may be able to [a]bear it.

WORSHIPPER THOUGHTS!

Do I encourage others?

___

___

___

___

Do I like to encourage others?

___

___

___

___

When was the last time I encouraged someone?

___

___

___

___

Community

And let us consider one another in order to stir up love and good works, not forsaking the assembling of ourselves together, as is the manner of some, but exhorting one another, and so much the more as you see the Day approaching.–Hebrews 10:24-25

Community

**A GROUP OF PEOPLE LIVING IN THE SAME PLACE
OR HAVING A PARTICULAR CHARACTERISTIC IN COMMON**

*Now I plead with you, brethren, by the name of our
Lord Jesus Christ, that you all speak the same thing, and that
there be no divisions among you, but that you be perfectly joined
together in the same mind and in the same judgment. –1 Corinthians 1:10*

Presently my community is Crown Ministries in Canarsie Brooklyn. In our community there are all types of people. Though there are different economic classes within communities, all can benefit from the worship of community. Giving back is a form of worship as we are helpers of one another. Crown Ministries is a community church where we try to reach those in our community both spiritually and naturally.

Spiritually we preach and teach the word of God, not just to the old or young, but to all who will receive it. We don't have a set demographic on who we'd like to touch. Our goal is to touch as many as possible. So we want everyone in our congregation to be community oriented. After church we gather outside like most churches do after a service, but it's encouraged that we speak to those who pass by, not just move to the side.

My husband, Dr. Shaw has walked through the housing development and all over our community to familiarize himself, and so, the community can familiarize itself with him. This is why I believe with all my heart our church is respected in the community. There was a drug dealer in our neighborhood that my husband always spoke to. They'd actually sit and talk about life, and why this young man chose the life he did. After many conversations with my husband this young man began to change his life. I didn't say he stopped completely, but he'd come to church, and encouraged others to come as well. The young became ill, and Dr. Shaw would pray for him and encouraged him to give his life to the Lord. Before that young man passed away, he was introduced to and accepted the Lord.

What would have happened if Dr. Shaw thought this young man wasn't worth a conversation because of his occupation as a drug dealer; if he would have allowed him to walk by and not commune with him? His family was blessed by the impact my husband had on him, they would often come to visit the church.

Every year Crown puts together a few events for our community.

Crown Fest – This is known as our Health and Education fair. Through partnerships, we provide health and education resources to the community. Several leaders and participants join us on this day to share their heart for the community. There are bouncy houses, basketball, entertainment, singing and overall fun for the entire family.

Thanksgiving – The Tuesday before Thanksgiving, we visit the shelter around the corner from our church and feed those who live there a wonderful dinner. We've also opened our church to feed the community on Thanksgiving morning. We don't assume everyone has a meal because we have one. We also give away bags of food, clothing, a turkey, and fresh veggies.

Open House – We invite people to visit other than a Sunday morning to know what we're about.

What else besides preaching goes on at Crown Ministries? Men's Ministry, Women's Ministry, Singles Ministry, Couples Ministry, Food and Clothing Pantry, and much more. Come by and visit us one Sunday. 1 Thessalonians 5:14 –Now we [a]exhort you, brethren, warn those who are unruly, comfort the fainthearted, uphold the weak, be patient with all.

WORSHIPPER THOUGHTS!

Am I community oriented?

_____

_____

_____

Do I give back to my community?

_____

_____

_____

Do I belong to a church that helps the community?

_____

_____

_____

Church Service
The Action of Helping or Doing Work for Someone

For a day in Your courts is better than a thousand. I would rather be a doorkeeper in the house of my God Than dwell in the tents of wickedness.
–Psalm 84:10

Fellowship is something, I was always told, is useful in your walk with God. Yes, there are many who believe the Television Evangelist is their Pastor, but there is no obligation from either side. The viewer is encouraged through the television, but what else are they committed to in the church. One hears the Sunday word, but what about the Bible Study? Is Sunday worship the only thing needed? Does it fulfill to the point of having enough ammunition against the enemy if he sends temptation? What happens when we've allowed non-church activities to take the place of Sunday worship; how then are you nourished?

Serving people is my passion; it's one of my places of comfort. Serving others is a hard thing for lots of people. Reason being, some people aren't nice. But when you share your church service with love and kindness, it will draw men. Personally, I don't mind the difficult people. As a matter of fact I prefer them, because it's my opportunity to show that I'm not doing this because I have to, it's because I love to. And when you love doing what you do in the house of God it shows up as an easy task. God should get the glory through your service of worship. We worship God by using our natural and spiritual gifts to serve others.

Again, serving people is my passion because when I wasn't singing, I served as an usher. Some people actually enjoy doing this and have made it their only job in the church. For me, I looked forward to putting on my white uniform and standing at my post. There was nothing like waiting for the people to come to service so I could greet and help them start their day off right.

I knew it was important for people to see a smiling and happy face when they came to the house of God. You never know what someone is going through at home or may have run into on their way to church. Therefore, it's important when serving, to have an attitude of worship. When we are at home worship is wonderful, but there's something about being with and serving other powerful believers that makes worship special.

WORSHIPPER THOUGHTS!

How do I serve in church?

_____

_____

_____

What ministry can I contribute to in church that will enhance it?

_____

_____

_____

Is my service limited to only when God shows up?

_____

_____

_____

Do I allow God to have full reign over my life?

CONNECTION

A RELATIONSHIP IN WHICH A PERSON, THING, OR IDEA IS LINKED OR ASSOCIATED WITH SOMETHING ELSE

Now I urge you, brethren, note those who cause divisions and offenses, contrary to the doctrine which you learned, and avoid them.
–Romans 16:17

A connection with the Father is what we all need in this life we live. Often we allow situations and circumstances to get in the way of that connection. For a moment we think of God as a regular man who owes us something. That is a moment of temporary insanity.

Within our walk with God, many of us (at one time or another), have allowed others to interrupt our connection and worship to God. But His word is clear on how to handle this. It says to keep a sharp eye out for those who take bits and pieces of the teaching that we've learned and then use them to make trouble. In other words, people who use tactics and tricks to pull us away from Him. It says to give them wide berth (adequate distance), because their intention is only to get out of you what they can.

Connect with someone who talks like you; a fellow worshipper. Know those who labor among you. You know what and who fits in your life. Choose the perfect fit.

Connect with your destiny. Ruth connected with her destiny when she took a chance to follow someone she grew to know and trust, in her mother-in law Naomi. After Naomi lost her husband and sons, she was left with two daughters-in-law. She couldn't produce anymore children; things were looking bad where she was so she decided to return to a place that was familiar to her. At first Ruth and Orpah decided to go with her, but Orpah changed her mind and decided to stay behind. But Ruth decided there was a connection there, and believed within herself that going with Naomi will help her find her destiny. Connection will have you in a place that favor will find you. Shout connection. I don't only want to connect with people; I want people to think that connecting with me is a blessing for them as well.

WORSHIPPER THOUGHTS!

Am I connected to the right people at work?

_____

_____

_____

Am I connected to the right people at church?

_____

_____

_____

Is there anyone in my life trying to separate me from connecting with God?

_____

_____

_____

Am I making destiny connections?

GIVING

FREELY TRANSFER THE POSSESSION OF SOMETHING TO SOMEONE

A man's gift makes room for him,
And brings him before great men. –Proverbs 18:16

Giving financially is definitely a form of worship. Do you give tithes and offering? Do you give cheerfully, willingly, or grudgingly? Do you give sacrificially? Do you give voluntarily? Where do you fall in all of this as an act of worship?

Giving is an expression of Love. "For God so loved the world that He gave his only begotten son". God was the biggest giver in giving His Son.

What do you give of yourself? Is giving only financial? Of course giving is not only financial. People give of themselves every day, some making sacrifices. Some give out of need and want, but there are others that give voluntarily to be a help to someone else.

Followers of Christ are givers who don't give to be seen by men. Our motives should be good, not seeking anything in return. What we do in secret, God will reward us openly. We must examine our hearts as givers.

Do you consult God before you give? We must ultimately please God in our giving. Speak to someone who was a tither and stopped tithing. You may hear some regret from them. We mustn't look at our tithe as helping the church budget, but view it as a thank you God offering. Again, giving is a form of worship. Is your worship abundant or inhibited? Are you getting a wealthy return, or is your return hindered? Jesus gave a costly sacrifice, His life. We don't want to be in the flow of giving just enough. Matthew 6:21 – For where your treasure is, there your heart will be also.

Worshipper Thoughts!

Do I give to be seen?

_____

_____

_____

Do I give with selfish motives?

_____

_____

_____

Do I give with the right heart?

_____

_____

_____

Is God pleased in the way I give?

_____

_____

_____

SUPPORT/LISTENING
TO BEAR ALL OR PART OF THE WEIGHT OF; HOLD UP

Bear one another's burdens, and so fulfill the law of Christ. –Galatians 6:2

This particular scripture hit home for me because I am learning more and more of what it means.

Are you a good/great supporter of your brother or sister? Are you your brother's keeper?

There was a man sick with palsy that couldn't get close to Jesus to ask for his healing, but he had some friends that understood his burden, and dug a hole in the roof of the house Jesus was in. They made sure their friend could get close to Jesus. They are a great example of how you help people get to worship. You support them and you lead them to Jesus, and the rest is up to them.

Understand your support to others should be intentional and positive. Your support says you believe in them. Having someone believe in you is priceless. There are those who will believe in you even when you don't believe in yourself.

Not only do we show support by believing in someone, we show it by listening to them. Supportive people are good listeners and sincere in our willingness to lend an ear. Helping someone stay on course goes a long way.

Worshipper Thoughts!

Am I supportive?

_____

_____

_____

How can I be more supportive?

_____

_____

_____

Am I a good listener?

_____

_____

_____

RESOURCES

A SUPPLY OF MATERIALS, STAFF AND OTHER ASSETS THAT CAN BE DRAWN ON BY A PERSON OR ORGANIZATION IN ORDER TO FUNCTION EFFECTIVELY
FOOD – ANY NUTRITIOUS SUBSTANCE THAT PEOPLE EAT OR DRINK IN ORDER TO MAINTAIN LIFE AND GROWTH

Is it not to share your bread with the hungry,
And that you bring to your house the poor who are cast out;
When you see the naked, that you cover him, And not hide yourself
from your own flesh? Then your light shall break forth like the morning,
Your healing shall spring forth speedily, And your righteousness shall
go before you; The glory of the Lord shall be your rear guard.
–Isaiah 58:7-8

When I read this scripture in the Message Bible, it brought me to tears of worship. The Lord is interested in seeing us share our food with the hungry. How often do we walk by the hungry without feeling bad that we did it? You know why, because we're eating. We are eating spiritually and naturally and don't see the hungry before us. It says we should invite the poor into our homes, put clothes on the shivering. We have coats in our closets that we can't fit, but won't take a moment to give them to someone who can use it. There are many that hold on to resources about employment and programs, which can help their family, friends, and fellow church members. A worshipper shares food, resources and strives to be a blessing. I'm not saying you shouldn't take care of yourself or should give from something you don't have, but it's important to take care of others in the capacity we can. According to the word, charity is the greater.

Do you know why I'm blessed the way I am, because I give clothes away, and my closet is replenished because of it. But that's not what really got me about this word; it's when it says "be available to your own families." You have family among you that need FOOD. They need nourishment. They are dying of hunger, and we have the ability to feed them, but we don't.

As a worshipper if we do what's right, our lives will turn around at once. It says that our righteousness will pave our way. The God of glory will secure your passage. Then when you pray, God will answer. His word says "You'll call out for help and I'll say, 'Here I am.' Don't you want God to hear your prayer?

I challenge you! If you see someone in need of a meal, feed them. I guarantee it will feed your soul. Proverbs 3:27 – Do not withhold good from those to whom it is due. When it is in the power of your hand to do so.

Worshipper Thoughts!

Do I freely give food if asked?

_____

_____

_____

Do I give out of my abundance?

_____

_____

_____

Do I know of resources and don't share them?

_____

_____

_____

Conclusion

Living The Life of a Worshipper appears to be a lot based on what you've just read. However, it's not. To live this life we should have the Lord in the forefront of our minds and hearts in all that we say and do. It also means to have and enjoy personal fellowship with the Lord.

In the life of worship, we see loving others (family, church, and community) can be the greatest example and bridge for many to get acquainted and form a solid relationship with God.

In living this life, we see there are many challenges one may encounter, but I can truthfully testify that challenges are lighter with the Lord.

We see, as we continue to strengthen our worship walk, we can have special moments of intimacy with God by praying, singing, moments of reflection, reading the word as well as hearing the preached word. To know we have all of this when we want and need it is a beautiful thing.

In living this life, the joy of the Lord is our strength where belief, fearlessness, patience and truth reign. We strive to live a life of humility, consistency and balance so that God may get the glory always.

Dear reader, all of the above works but doesn't work if have not confessed Christ as your Lord and Savior. I cannot assume because you are reading this book, you are saved.

If you're not, you can do it right now simply by stating…

> *Lord Jesus*
> *Come into my life*
> *Forgive me of my sins*
> *I confess with my mouth*
> *I believe in my heart*
> *That Christ Jesus was born*
> *He died*
> *And is coming back again*
> *For me*
> *I no longer belong to the devil, but now belong to God*
> *And now I'm Saved.*

Hallelujah! You are now saved. If you were already saved, there's nothing wrong with confessing Christ once more. Now it's time we give praise and thanksgiving to God for deliverance from death.

1-6 *I love GOD because he listened to me,*
   listened as I begged for mercy.
He listened so intently
   as I laid out my case before him.
Death stared me in the face,
   hell was hard on my heels.
Up against it, I didn't know which way to turn;
   then I called out to GOD for help:

"Please, GOD!" I cried out.
   "Save my life!"
GOD is gracious — it is he who makes things right,
   our most compassionate God.
GOD takes the side of the helpless;
   when I was at the end of my rope, he saved me.
7-8 I said to myself, "Relax and rest.
   GOD has showered you with blessings.
   Soul, you've been rescued from death;
   Eye, you've been rescued from tears;
   And you, Foot, were kept from stumbling."
9-11 I'm striding in the presence of GOD,
   alive in the land of the living!
I stayed faithful, though bedeviled,
   and despite a ton of bad luck,
Despite giving up on the human race,
   saying, "They're all liars and cheats."
12-19 What can I give back to GOD
   for the blessings he's poured out on me?
I'll lift high the cup of salvation — a toast to GOD!
   I'll pray in the name of GOD;
I'll complete what I promised GOD I'd do,
   and I'll do it together with his people.
When they arrive at the gates of death,
   GOD welcomes those who love him.

Oh, GOD, here I am, your servant,
  your faithful servant: set me free for your service!
I'm ready to offer the thanksgiving sacrifice
  and pray in the name of GOD.
I'll complete what I promised GOD I'd do,
  and I'll do it in company with his people,
In the place of worship, in GOD's house,
  in Jerusalem, GOD's city.
Hallelujah!

Psalm 116 (MSG)

God Bless You!!!

www.ingramcontent.com/pod-product-compliance
Lightning Source LLC
Chambersburg PA
CBHW081155290426
44108CB00018B/2561